VERSES FROM A MORTAL SOUL

ANURAG NATH

To all those who inspired me,

And to my dear muses.

Contents

Preface

This collection comes forth to explore the emotions of the mortal soul. The fate of mankind that follows today is but a sorrowful one and most of my works tend to reflect this melancholy may it be through the lens of existentialism or through the spiralling abyss of thoughts one might find within themselves.

As we move forward to a more technologically advanced society, we find the art of poetry writing being reduced to an algorithmic output. In such a perilous time, I wish to seek the true lantern passed down through the ages of literature, upon whose light, the human soul sings the poems born of emotions. And as we stand at the very end of the path, an era of uncertainty gloomed by unknown shadows, awaits us ahead. So as I present, *"THE VERSES FROM A MORTAL SOUL"*, I aim to remind the world, that poetry born from human experience, emotions and inspirations, remains unparalleled. Once Wordsworth argued for the natural beauty of poetry, free from artificial ornamentation, and my anthology embodies this sentiment. Each poem in this collection, has been shaped by songs, shows, incidents, history, events and individuals, or imagined truths, that have ignited my soul. This collection hence, is the true reflection, of what I have felt, perceived and understood, which is presented in the most vivid of colours, through the art of poetry.

1. Maple Leaves

Upon the edge of the cliff of life I stand,
Tomorrow they shall push me off into the abyss.
Today I am capable enough to fight,
But from tomorrow I'm naught.

Once I was 11, innocent and blessed,
Amidst the tranquil green, unafraid and unlettered.
Untouched by fate's spiked cactus,
Dancing upon the echoes of joy and laughter.

Once I was 17, young and spirited,
Traded my youthful desires for ambition's roar.
Living upon the arrogance of father's fame,
Learning to live in the past of happy childhood days.

Once I was 24, zealous and hardworking.
Bore the heavy weight of promises made,
To ailing parents who had started to fade
All their sacrifices for me, and yet nothing could I barter,
For they had already lost their pleasant desires.

Once I was 28, romantic and handsome,
Now heated by those pleasures I gave up then.
Drinking and feasting upon risqué beauties,
Living the delusion of the best moments in life.

Once I was 42, a father and a hero of sorts,
I was the champion, and I was their god.
I carried the weights of those trustful eyes,
Their expectations were now my goals,
And my dream was to make them smile.

Once I was 51, weary and a tortured soul,
My promoted ranks taking their toll,
My soul cried in silence for my lavish life.
My bones weren't able to carry the stress.
Yet for my family I walked straight ahead.

Once I was 58, the final guide of my child.
The dreams in his eyes yelled at my thoughts.
Tireless did I strife for his inception.
Realising my own parents' sacrifices,
Ungrateful to have never pleased their souls.

Now I'm 59, upon the edge of the cliff of employment,
They shall push me into the abyss of retirement and I shall fall.
Today my inner eyes opened wide,
My love for working instilled deep within.
Tomorrow shall force me to become that jobless useless man,
I was afraid of becoming when I was 17.

Thus I pray my gods to heed,
And hence I sit still in the darkness of solitude,
Begging to meet my busy child once a month,
For I am that hopeless, useless, worthless man.
My deeds are a burden, and my thoughts are now of the
madman's.

So swiftly did it turn to falling Maple,
Don't get closer to my crisp insanity I beg,
Soon I shall be blown by the winds of autumn,
Only my Krishna shall now save me from hell.

2. Essence of the Bard

Falling are the petals of rhyme,
A new age now thrives aloud,
Singing to the old rhythm yet,
Dancing to a lyric-less sound.

Since before Jesus was acclaimed,
A Bard walked through these plains,
Denouncing the world to create his own,
His songs, the automobile to his abode.

When Colosseums were built to echo the brute,
The Bard sang in taverns aloof,
And even when all rejoiced upon battles,
They taught their children of the lyrical first.

Against the populated infection he went,
The Bard's journey, a sorrowful tale,
Sometimes fighting the heroes,
Other times losing to the villains alike.

Watering the earth with his tears,
Ripening the crops to his hymn,
Presenting the very jest of this world,
Singing on winds of the forsaken turf.

First the Epics came forth to shine,
Tales not of himself lone anymore,
Lonely as he has been throughout,
The Bard now had friends,
To sing along the Canterbury way.

But perchance they captured the Bard there,
Renouncing him back to reality,
Struggled in agony as he was repleted then,
But in this lonely cage his sorrow did aid
To bring alive the sweetest fourteen lines!

Imprisoned he was now homesick,
And the Angels disregarding all his calls,
Yet from the depths Lucifer did hear him pray,
Mephistopheles was hence summoned to doctor,
The Bard then cursed forevermore.

Freed from his reigns he again denounced,
To go back home, where Paradox was born,
People finally comprehending to some extent,
But Metaphysical still it was to them,
For the Bard's conceit was yet not plain.

Recovered he was now healthy,
His most glorious period began to leak,
The cursed Bard hence now did write,
Of how the man had lost the Paradise.

The demon's elixir then taking its toll,
So the Bard went back to the classics for a cure,
Now a Deserted Village did here lay,
While the Bard was absent from his caves.

Finally discovering the cure in traditionals,
The Bard then finally returns to nature,
Where he sang of verses so romantic,
Dancing along with Daffodils and singing with Nightingales.

Whilst soothing broken hearts with red roses,
The people ignored the lad who called himself a Bard,
And again he Wandered lonely as a cloud,
Yet smiling like in his mediaeval past.

To end him even Lucifer did fail,
Bad times are never an omen,
The vision is the very muse that shines,
Upon his abode he still resides.

3. The Winter Rain

The cold shower of the winter night,
Freezes my soul's burning appetite.
For to her I succumb and flow to ends,
Sweet is the scent of every bough in rain.

The first drizzle is a chill of amazement,
The youthful play of teasing to sensation.
Dripping through my skin, a spark to seed,
Her drops falling prey to my thirsty leads.

Slowly does she soak me in colours so wet,
Bleeding through the clouds with heavied breaths.
Colder I get with every touch she extends,
To every drop of personality I drown abed.

The hibiscus unfolds slowly to embrace,
To the colourless night it mingles to breed,
Warm are the screams of bliss, to the winter cold.
No lightning but only sweet drops to hold.

Then colder she gets, the drops of rain,
Each trying to freeze my heart inlaid.
The shower of love accepting my roses,
Every petal now heavier than the thorns of bite.
Drenched to her, I bore her within,
The winter rain of the moonlit night.

4. Journey of the Cursed I

PART I - The Gambit of the Curse

Infront they stood of colossal might,
Though scared to bones, they didn't fright.
For love doth conquer evil they had heard,
A thousand suns on their skin yet burnt.
Was he hotter than Apollo, this fiend?
This horror from legends, once again redeemed.

Though cornered, the son of El Diablos still was complacent,
Bred of blood so malicious and hated.
Though all his trickery and might must have failed,
For the chosen two were now standing on his face!
But why fear? He is the Demon Lord,
The Devil that looms upon terror's might.
Tossing his necro sword afar for the ritual,
His dripping thick blood upon his palm he raises.
He prays, or does he? No! he curses,
The ritual of horror he does practices.

"Demon it is thy end!" Cries the man with a holy roar!
"We have come to slay you!" Echoes his beloved through
evermore.
"No magic shall save you from our might
For blessed we are from all that you fright!"
But why would the Infernal Lord pay them with heed?
Hence he begins with his voice so thunderous and haughty.

"To the dungeons I call, heed my say!
For I am the epitome, on which you doth prey,
To my command you listen and make use of thy life,
To me, the prince of hell, you all must pay the price.
Hence kindle the hell's pyre and let Gaia's skin bubble and
seethe,
Scorching the holy grail, ashen the humans and bastards for
feast.
These ashes are hence sacrifices to raise,
For I summon the Grand King, the ruler of rage.
Upon whose might even the gods do break!
Outcasts from Babylon tonight shall banquet.
For he comes to strengthen his blooded ghouls in debt,
I call thee my Lord of Nemesis, through the ends of time,
Satan the only boon of horror, crowned by the voids!"

Panicked they watched him with fear,
As the blood flames wrapped him in their care.
Uranus so old now, still did remember,
Ages ago when Satan once did conquer.
Haphaestus awestruck shouted through Olympus,
"It is the end, we did fail yet again to conquer!"

Taking from even the deeds of mankind,
From the very hatred bred of the human soul and slander,
He calls his Satan upon the humane abode to conquer.
Artemis too did rage upon this horror,
"Why must mankind be so heartless and unbothered!?"

"For the sun shines upon them as it must, Artemis,
For the moon isn't delayed by her stars.
Whenever they prayed we did listen,
So our dear children now have taken us for grant"
Sorrow filled Apollo's burning heart,
The sun's so pale now, cold in its stark.

"Betrayed they have us Zeus,
But had you not foresee this disgrace?
I beg to pardon this spite, but as you may see,
The blood flames now surround, our couple doth he shames!"

Hermes cries, watching them in his tricky remake.
"Oh listen Zeus! Hear him chant!
Now who shall save the world from his plans!?"

"Thy fear is understood, but thy will so unjustified Hermes,
Why must thee breed such thoughts so foul?
We are yet to see the Darklord arising from his bough?
Why must you make such thoughts in haste?"
Calm he sat still, oh the greater one,
A little hum on the clouds, perhaps his patience.

Ares so enthralled, and in panic,
"These quakes are nothing like Poseidon's tectonic.
Such energy, so bombarding and destructive,
You must be in immense pain dear Gaia!
Cronus thy must heed this doom and egress,
It is thy mother who is burning in hell's charade!"

"Osiris you see this? The flames from hell doth rage!"
"The souls here crying in terror this doomsday,
They wish not to leave us yet Anubis, and your scales do shake,
But can we even protect the tranquil souls from such flames!?"

While the couple in fright still stood on their power,
"You must be bluffing us! Satan cannot be summoned at this
hour!"
"But the ritual he chants, the mantras of hatred,
What is it dear love Hazel if not a call to his favorite?"

The flames engulfing the demon doth protects,
No might now has the strength to chariot.
To even lay a scratch on that beast as he chants,
His gore hence smiles upon the helpless man.

There beyond the horizon a tandav begins,
Shiva prepares to dance upon the Infernal Flames,
Once he begins can even Vishnu stop him?
The dance of the doom, the dream of the end.

"But Orario we must do something with haste,
This can't be how it is fated to fail!"
Orario upon himself doth takes the blame,
"If only I were stronger to end Satan himself this day!"
They hold hands tight, their fingers entangled to pleasure,
Awaiting to meet their doom by the demon's measure
"Gods of heaven you must peer!
Named in many but I see you are scared!

We, your chosen children await the doom in face,
While you await with us like our comrades who bled!
The ego of mankind you didn't slay,
Such dismay on my Hazel's shoulders you indeed have placed.
And now you watch! And doth watch only from thy abode
among realms!"

❧❧❧

"Oh hush Orario they are as helpless I say,
For they mustn't intervene in the human reigns!
But Darling look! We together in pure light do gaze.
The Gods so far from us in their cosmic base,
But we the doves fighting the one they so fear to face.
While I pity those that upon the Colosseum must take their
shrines,
While having the charisma of cosmetic heavenly designs!
But until I hold your soul within my gaze,
Nothing doth matters, neither the gods nor the demon we face.

❧❧❧

But there the demon grins and oh what a horrific one was it!
Is it but prepared and ready to breach the fathom of Hell?
"Thine burning blood is what I seek,
Let me be the best of thy majestic breed!"
Astonished then, Hermes doth wonders,
"Where is it Zeus? The Demon Lord of Pandemonium, I ponder?

❧❧❧

Osiris' deep sigh says it all so crystal,
The souls, finally in relief do gather to wonder.
"Did it fail?" Marveled the Guardian of the Scales.
Shiva finally took to his seat in solace,
But something was wrong he knew in that face!
Why Vishnu was still with such horrible stress?

Then wishful the demon doth presents the gift,
A drop of the very blood of his father's creed,
"I knew it! Satan's evil is but not for tonight.
It is but a drop of blood, he prays,
Orario we must make haste for his head to slaughter!
The couple in charge, held their blades with honour.

To their approach the demon but snickers
In his voice so foul, with demonic breath he whispers,
"With it you shall bend to me at long last,
My omnipresence thereby forever fulfilled!"
Devouring the drop in haste he declares,
"I, the son of Satan hereby curses thy fates!"

"Do you realise this song's tone alas, Hermes?
Oh children of Olympus, witness together to bear,
A fierce curse boiled of Satan's vivid lyre!
A sheen drop of woe rolls down her sight,
Artemis couldn't hold her moon's final light.

Uranus still steadfast, sweats and awaits,
His Gaia half roastedd in hell's burning blaze.
Hence the world did quake again but on Poseidon's will,
So much for holding back his senses of avid.

"Tonight's moon is but the last you together sip,
For henceforth you must forever heed my say,
The distance is but the length of a Titan's embrace,
And perchance you get closer to another's sight,
One shall be at bed by your conqueror's side.
So run now, make haste with your virgin fear,
For thy Apollo shall rise without wiping his tears."

5. Journey of the Cursed II

PART II - *The Fire of Hope*

Decades after decades had slipped in mist,
Clouded was hell, upon memory of one the other did breathe.
Etched upon blood with sickening blood itself,
Bright red it burnt at times of distress.
The marks forever enchaining the doves,
The curse imprisoned their warm scent of love.
A brand of infinite weights they now do carry,
A tattoo to declare their cursed creed of unholy.

They carved on stones and scratched upon woods,
Left messages for their separated souls on wounds,
Incarcerated to live was perhaps a punishment to fail,
For that red demon still upon the lands did hail.
To trick the gods would be to fulfill the curse,
When one doth flies to that reaper of thirst,
But none did know who the demon upon whimsical play,

Would pick and fly to his Pandemonium cave.

❧❧❧

Here the Yeuleus shores of greenery are now in grey,
The forest soil for Orario was but a doll to break.
Anguish still burned in his blood with rage,
Was he blaming himself yet again? Or perhaps his Gods for this
fate?
Alas when Artemis had tried to console,
His eyes had spoken louder than his defeated soul.
Till then it is but Hermes who dares a day or two,
Singing him songs to cultivate his mood,
But to his lyrics Orario was heavily displeased.
Staring at the ground he had stared for years,
Asking the singer about his inspirational notion.

❧❧❧

"To the dragon's dripping blood Icarus had melted,
For the cause had Rehleus fallen to the abyss.
Their haunting eyes upon my life they peer,
Their hopes within me...within us, to fulfill the quest of demonic
fear,
Those befallen comrades at thousands in the phantom hole,
And I weep and weep but not a drop for their anguished souls,
All I weep is for her, my darling living abroad at the foreign
shores.
Then why am I to listen to your songs of grief,

Why are they not sung as I am by you Hermes?
Have I yet not wronged them enough, you still believe!?"

෴෴෴

Upon the heavy heart of Olympus there sat,
The God lord so silent in his thoughtful disguise.
"Zeus! Let them but join my boat to serenity,
Is it your will to breed but a brother to Satanic affinity!?
I am but the lone one, on whose care they perhaps shall rest,
Let them be at peace, for they have suffered enough distress."

෴෴෴

From his gloom of cosmic thoughts unknown,
A whisper it was or perhaps in tune,
"This is but not how it is to end, Anubis of scales,
There is much yet left to their obsessive fates,
Do you not hear that far song wind of trickery,
That mocks my rule yet craves me to not take my step."
Three hundred and seventy years had bested,
But there was yet more left to be tested.

෴෴෴

But there stood Hazel's statue with forever tears,
Ones that flowed from Salacia's welled up pools.
Watering the lake at her feet,
Nightmares upon nightmares she did heedfully desire.
All the brethren, the soldiers burnt to the char,

They questioned her before the end of the moonlit hour,
The quest unfulfilled, their souls at unrest took to gloom,
The black lotus upon her heart they watered to bloom.
But she with her last bravery did embrace the nightly horror,
For it was the only time when she upon his face could gaze.
Though hollow to the eyes that were so flushed,
To the gray and black tunes of the deceased mush.

Hence upon the chilly breeze of Kailash,
Ganesha did ask Athena to empower,
The God of war to blaze the spirit of two in cold.
"But why must I bless them with such false hope?"
To Athena's rightful question he then smiled,
"It is no false imagery that is to blind,
But with all honesty they must be prepared,
For Hercules has reached the mountain top to labour,
The frozen wheel of fate is yet again to travel,
The Immortal Titan of benevolence rises again resilient,
To help our couple struggling with Satanic lesion."

To enrage the man raged within was but tranquil,
Athena's was the warcry that mobilized his mental grave.
What Hermes saw was but a miracle in consciousness of gold,
As Orario's eyes after hundreds of years again sparkled with hope.
But to pluck the parasite of grief, the lotus in black,

From her heart soiled by miserable nightly smoke,
For Athena to wake up Hazel's embedded devoured soul.

"Hear me child of heavenly principles,
It is but time again for you to remember,
The vows made and the glory inherited within.
They all look forward to that break of spring,
So freeze it not upon sorrowful tears,
Let the heroic flames burn against your fear.
For he comes to strengthen his children of clay,
Hence You and Orario shall yet again face,
To end the rule of that demonic disgrace!
Oh look there he rises, the benevolent thief,
Can you hear that Titan breathing with grief?
This is the chance, the one and only,
To fight again that demon so malevolent.
And perhaps the tattoo of grief shall fade,
To the drumming beats of your winning success!"

Upon the final eve when the sun was but hung low,
Their lighted a warm fire orange and red,
A miracle of divinity had them blessed,
The Guardian of Humanity to finally come on-board.
He who had watched the tormented tale in snow,
While caged he was for gifting the fire from heaven's bough.

6. Journey of the Cursed III

Part III – The Burden of Gods

Upon the morning sun so bright,
There came the Titan liberator white.
To break the rhythm followed till night,
The ballad of gloomy grey perilous tides.
To shoulder the weights marked in flares,
To break the rules for the heartfelt prayer.

From Tartarus' caves awakened the father,
A purple eminence, sinister hence caged,
Wishing to witness the final songs of the world.
Seclusion's prison of sanctity withholds,
Even the villains died of forgotten sands,
Were ready to behold the grand scheme at stance.

Athena's roar had quaked their souls,
Ganesha's promise of enlightenment withholds.
As Zeus watches the final act to unfold,
Apollo shines brighter than ever before.

Upon the cosmic abode where consciousness flows,
A break of vision, there Vishnu gazes,
Peering upon the children he doth praises,
The couple unfurling their hearts unfazed,
Forever engraved on the historical citadel,
The Couple of the Curse to finally make,
Their last stand against the Satanic reign.

But oh look there! The demon grins,
Doth he think of mocking upon tuned lyrics,
His soul casts shameless thoughts of foul breed,
Such pride upon the curse of his father's creed,
Gothic he walks with the cane of confidence.
His lair upon iced caves beheld his fulfillment.
Where lava flows through and through,
And yet stands cold ice tall and crude,
Such persona of demonic display,
Honour fills and chugs every mug of presumptuous prey.

Till the far stretched ends of the horizon's bay,
The repear of decay has walked incessant.
The stench of dead no more in the air,
For Ninlil passed without a breath to share,
And the charcoal of souls was itself the air.

Yet choked Eurus, came to guide,
Orario's steps till the towering sight.
While Zephyrus guided Hazel to care,
Taking her to the lair of fearful nightmares.
But the Titan walked lone and by himself,
Anger controlled in his big brows that frowned.

Each step, a pain to the aura itself,
Oh how life has suffered these rotting years.
Will any prayer save them from the curses of the souls that
passed,
Those men who believed in the heroes till the midnight hour.
The petals within do start to dance,
Upon the murmur of these Cursed lands,
Where sorrow embraces to soiled fertility,
A part forever lost to his demonic cruelty.

Tethys' soul looked void of emotions,
Passing her gaze was a horrific intrusion.
Half chared and her purity imbued with burns,
Yet the she stood still and mature not shunned.
While Gaia's strength to withhold the pyre of hell,
The mother against the demon's firey wrath did roar,
More than three hundred years, and she still fought without fear.

There stood the demon on his towering balcony,
Facing his guest who had stomped to his hive,
Prometheus looked through the demon's heartless eyes.
No fear to face the reaper of lands, the monster of hell,
Only a sorrowful flame did burn against his soul that cried.

To the far right of the mighty Titan blew,
Chilly winds across Orario's temples.
A bubble of rage upon the breeze did fly,
As he could see the fiend afar on that tower of might.
But there burst the bubble, to the sensation aloof,
A feel of her grief far to the horizon's boon,
He knew she had come but with broken tunes.

Still stoned in her moves, and quenched,
For the soul that now was closer yet not her's hold.
A heavy tear did roll and broke the lands upon it fell,
As she saw the fiend up on the tower of hell,
Who smiled witnessing the pain, the suffering he had dealt.

"Such cruelty upon the man, the souls unrest",
The frustrated indignant Titan proclaimed.
"The rivers now are but purple and crimson like thy self!
Oh! Burnt you not a single foliage, but,
Choked you did to their decaying deaths!
The lands itself repel your stench,
Your sins too heavy for Gaia to bear,
And Tethys could never wash your soul,
But perhaps his lightning could end your cry,
Alas thou mustn't be relieved from thy shackles,
To that end, they did send these children of mine,
With whom you have played till that broken night,
But this shall be the new dawn of peace,
An end to you and your sinister crows unwinged!"

The smiling ghoul, now did laugh,
to the brave Titan's annoying wrath,
"A head so huge with a mindless brain,
Oh what jokes you crack, the Titan thief!"

Then ominous giggles went following to question,
"My end you say!? Boasting too hard for the thief you are!
I say try it, use those hands mighty and big,
And perhaps even those big feet if you wish!
Oh now I understand, them being the audience to it,
To witness it all, as I break your bones and thy teeth,
And I dare thee, the Titan, the benevolent thief!
But beg me not when I gouch thine eyes,
One for each of your cursed child!"

"Accepted are mistakes, from the son of Satan,
But I wish for you not to be a fool so true,"
Mocks the Titan unfazed by his words of truculence.
"Why would I take the fight that belongs,
The war that had started long past gone.
Hence my children who started this tale,
Shall bring you to this legend's fateful end,
And as I shall witness their bravery for myself,
Rejoiced I will be for their undefeated prayers.

"These two? The couple divided in bond and in strength?
Oh the funny Titan boasts even more nonsense!
They are but divided by my curse, in strength and divine,
What makes you believe they can defeat my glorious might?"
Royal was his laugh, but cruel did it sound,

Echoing through the valleys, the decaying grounds.

"Promise you I shall, that when it's done,
Thy cries shall crackle louder than thy laughs!
For I am the breaker of your chains of power,
To end the curse upon the doves, my children of love.
So here I present a Titan's embrace",
He says, lifting his arms, up and ahead,
"The father of benevolence I am, and I cannot see,
So their suffering shall burn to the ends that I hold!"
And from his palms sparkled flames orange and gold,
Then off they burnt till his shoulders that hold,
A Titan's arms now forever charcoaled.
Blowing a sigh of pain, and cries that he couldn't roll,
"A Titan's embrace, now reduced to none,
Dear children, do end him before he can run!"

Bewildered the doves, were shocked to behold,
The sight they had just witnessed so bold,
A few tears they did shed, unknowing,
For sorrow or for the joy of release from cages so cold.
Alas they must bear another soul, a Titanic weight to hold,
Hence with heavy hearts, heavier than stones,
They jumped and ran towards the demon now sold.

There the demon did now sweat, colder and red,
Hundreds of years and he still was afraid,
Frustrated his rage, he did shoot,
A beam of purple thundering disgrace,
Towards the now smiling Titan Prometheus.
But swift were they, the couple to come,
Blocking the attack on mist laden blades.
As each step took them closer to face,
Closer they got to themselves, with heavied breaths,
And their tears melted to mingle in a beloved embrace.

❧❧❧

Then "Demon it is thy end!" Cries the man with a holy roar!
"We have come to slay you!" Echoes his beloved through
evermore.
"No magic shall save you from our might
For blessed we are from all that you fright!"
A change of fates, aura enslaved,
The demon now starts to run away instead.

❧❧❧

Chasing the son of El Diablos, the couple,
Hand in hand, and blades craving to ends,
They charged behind the demon of Pandemonium.
In a flee of thoughts it was then,
When the disgraceful son thought to return.

Then with all his speed he did run to live,
Towards the portal that would save his creed.
And perhaps for a moment the couple did think,
They might lose the demon again and sin,
But alas as the demon did reach the portal of hell,
Loki stood there to smile to his pale white face,
Closing the portal with godly strength,
He made me a proud father that beautiful instance.

❧❧❧

Then went through the demon and his soul so foul,
Pure blades that cut through his heart and found,
An end to his demonic unworthy crown.
And as white flames erupted the demon did cry.
Then out went Apollo to come to enlight,
And God's golden flames wrapped the demon of night.
Echoing through lava and ice alike,
Were then his cries of devilish heights,
The Demon then perished with uncountable sins to life.

❧❧❧

And there they smiled, each God with relief and sigh,
As even the lands decayed did dance,
And a shower of serenity did enhance to enchant.
On a blissful moment, were the couple who finally held,
Each other to a kiss of true love's pleasing embrace.
And out they took their blades behind,

Each piercing through their loved soul with smiles,
Their lives forever now freed to fly,
For perhaps they couldn't bear to it, not a moment more,
And as their deed fulfilled, they finally took the rest they won.

Epilogue – The Overseer's Quill

So hence I record upon the branch itself,
Yggdrasil shall forever remember the world now shaped.
To be faithful and reliant enough to carry the weights,
The buurden of Godly cosmic reigns to hold,
For the cycle of life to move forward and for us to behold!

The couple in peace now do sleep together,
Reunited and relieved, they were unbound,
From the Godly gifts, to the souls now still,
From the wars that ravaged, to the Satanic will.

So I pray you mortals to once again remember,
The duty by grace and the virtue that binds -
To live, for it matters, and for those left behind.
For thy life was earned at prices so immortal,
And it would do thee good to respect the Journey of the Cursed
Couple.

- Odin, The Keeper of Fates

7. Crimson Fiction

To stand straight is but a fiction,
The eyes could never behold such honour.
The man leeches beyond streams of blood,
His appetite craves for tortured love.

Falling through the clouds of sin,
He drowns in decrypted horror's pool.
Wherein he observes with broken eyelids,
Sire Death busy at its work so cruel.

Pain could not measure his alarming agony,
It all had leaked through the cracks upon.
Nothing but echoes of vacuum did ring,
And empty stood his forever soul.

The night guides his freak within,
Limitless the man, a progeny of oblivion.
Blinded are the hopeful rays of the sun,
Why the saviour must rest behind a veil of fog?

Cleaved are his thoughts within, or,
Perhaps the man himself is now in two?
Who shall atone for those stains?
Or is it his fate yet again at fault?

The hymn of life begs for mercy,
I bet misery is what it shall see.
Was hearing to plead ever an aid?
For clean was the cut ever made to any throat.

The greasy black rain dares depict,
He couldn't care less for depictions ever still.
The last shower is on its doom,
No apocalypse shall come to save his boon.

He can't stand upright, the crimson criminal,
His sinister self upon hatred looms.
Rejection was already rejected from his care,
He upon the world now shall forever stare.

Playing the violin to the solemn oath,
Carrying himself to the graves evermore.
Degenerated his psycho fiction now shrieks,
Washing his hands of his brethren's soul.

His blood has hence gone thicket,
Though his skin stretches weaker still.
He spreads his wings so bleached throughout,
Pale feathers dancing upon graveyard silhouette.

Where shall he be brought to an end?
Who shall end the man within?
Is it a bait to breed another fiction?
Or perhaps the man shall forever ruin?...

8. My Lilac Dandelion

Long since the picture I portrayed,
Memory is a shackle that embraced,
Bottled upon a sweet blue blue day,
Heats the winter winds of damsel grey.

Reminiscing those eyes that snatched my gaze,
Pearls not unique in colours but shape.
So sharp yet so unfazed I was amazed,
Prettily set upon Chloris' best made.

The dandelion so soft to feel but zeal,
Yet enigma she carried of a child in play.
A flower to phoenix's beautiful flames,
I longed to feel that warmth, up close I prayed.

Traditional was her attire on that blue blue day,
White and red to a seraphic euphoria,
A smile perchance and I was dreaming to date,
Who won't be awestruck by such a serene bait?

To my surprise I then did learn,
My Dandelion's receptacle, lilac it burnt.
Not sinister but perhaps it craved gothic?
Modern to taste, I witnessed another face.

Revolted by chirping from birds and vales,
Yet I craved to burn by her lilac flares.
To the brink of sanity I was fleeting in self.
Dreams upon wonderlands and drinking till pale,
Dreaming of both, craving I was to haul her ever close.

Intoxication's cureless to the poison of love,
It's not the black rose I could betray in a gush.
Oh save me and let me burn to purple ashes,
My Lilac Dandelion charioting me to edges.

Traditional flames of pure red garlands her passion,
While the lilac flickering to her alluring sensations.
Losing my mind, the skies are so blue blue, why?
The dandelion in lilac was breathing my highs.

Echoing were thoughts so mingled then,
Distant were the sparkles and petals in flame.
Yet warmed I felt of heated pleasure and appeals,
An embrace I never had from my dandelion's feel.

Laughing to myself, I cried from within,
Lost my footing on life's Garden of Eden.
Was it me? That man in, faces so dramatic?
To submission, my lust to love pains likewise.

To gently pluck upon her petals with care,
The scent she graved within moments of prayer.
The flower on winds of summer kissed heat,
Favourite child of sunshine, her smile doth gleams.

To suffer from memories rooted to trees of intellect,
Why am I the prey to such beautiful incidents?
The lilac calls closer to my dandelion in white,
Helpless I wait, since that blue blue night...

9. The Last Nightingale

The last winds yonder a strong breeze,
Carrying the familiar upon its back.
Ribbons in symphony to the dew,
Nightingale's final ride comes at last.

The branches of intelligence I envisioned,
The cascade of insidious shadows fleeted.
Bytes received and taken to create,
Oh built the heaven upon this plate.

The crystals glow in radium green,
Passionate purple of the cyber fiend.
Such smog of horror it doth cleaves,
Flickering pale to the branches clean.

The basalt soot marbled to heat,
Glass that reflects our sinister feat.
Sky-less dystopia craves to fly,
The Immortal singer inspires every sigh.

To find dirt upon metal sleeves,
Growing the Oak that nests her creed.
Her last swoon, don't lose this day,
Her rainy song breaks sickly fays.

Drugged by greed's ambitious sail,
The future of loom together we hail.
Purity of the serene hopeless awaits,
Having her faith in our shameless games.

To grow with love is but tonight,
Loveless the titanium's fibrous might.
Titanic sank with heavied life,
Now frozen is the hull of venomous rife.

If black it grows by poisonous streams,
Smearing I believe in the frozen beams.
You crystal it not upon warming life,
The Immortal dies of dooming fife.

Not natural, upon intellectual bronchus,
She tunes her eyrie of clerical circus.
Failed to care, she cures our cancer,
Keats' nightingale comes to dreamers.

Author's Note

I write and write, and write some more,
For in the end, they shall breathe my life when I'm no more.

Hello readers,

Glad you could make it till the end! I hope some of the verses could touch your soul and connected to you. This is my first ever published book, and I'm really rejoiced about it, for in it are these poems that I have written through a period of time where I have felt different emotions through different times. Inspirations gained from songs and sagas, people and environment, imaginations and the world itself. While some verses were born from sleepless nights, others from the jump of a fleeting thought. Whether it is the againg of health, the fire of rebellion or the cold shower of love - each piece carries the echo of a lived moment, an emotion or an imaginary dance that stuck to me. I'm no sage with the answers to life, rather through these poems I carry questions to life, disguised by rhythm and rhyme. And even if a single stanza could touch your soul or mirror something deep within your heart, then happy I am, for my verses could do their part.

About The Author

Anurag Nath is an ardent writer and a poet with a love for exploring themes of tragedy, human emotions and nature. He is a student of English Literature who is inspired by mythical lore and modern sorrow alike. His imagery delves deeply into the human exprience, often reflecting upon the flaws of mankind. When not writing he enjoys sketching or making real-life short films.